# Table of Contents

We are learning about the United States.

I have a map of the
country.   It is **blank**.

I will fill in the map. I will label all 50 states!

I will also put a **compass rose** on the map.

A compass rose shows the four directions. They are
north, east, south, and west.

| | | | | |
|---|---|---|---|---|
| Alabama | Hawaii | Massachusetts | New Mexico | South Dakota |
| Alaska | Idaho | Michigan | New York | Tennessee |
| Arizona | Illinois | Minnesota | North Carolina | Texas |
| Arkansas | Indiana | Mississippi | North Dakota | Utah |
| California | Iowa | Missouri | Ohio | Vermont |
| Colorado | Kansas | Montana | Oklahoma | Virginia |
| Connecticut | Kentucky | Nebraska | Oregon | Washington |
| Delaware | Louisiana | Nevada | Pennsylvania | West Virginia |
| Florida | Maine | New Hampshire | Rhode Island | Wisconsin |
| Georgia | Maryland | New Jersey | South Carolina | Wyoming |

This is a list of all the state names.

A computer will help me
find each state's **location**.

# Completing a Map

I labeled Washington first.

Next, I labeled Florida.

It is tricky to label the smaller states.

Hawaii and Alaska are far away from the other states.

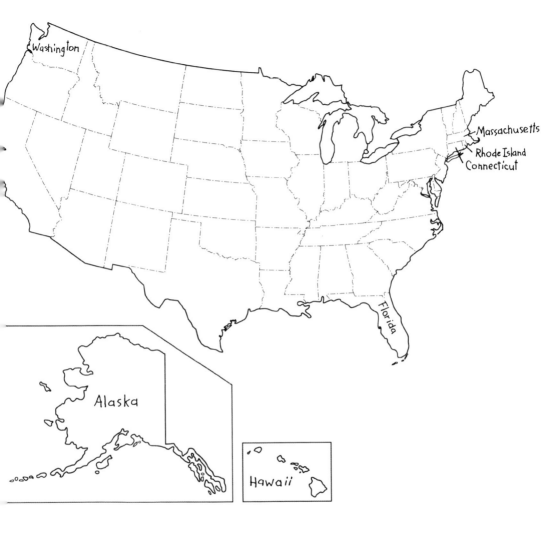

They have special spots on my map.

I colored the states I have visited blue.

I colored states I want to
visit green.

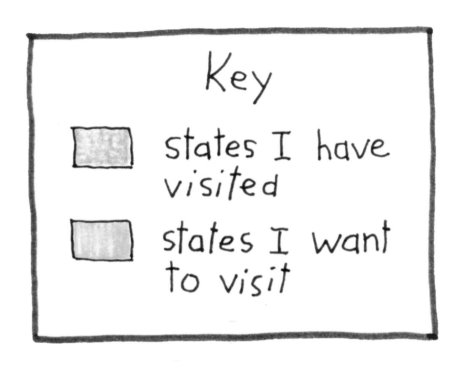

I made a map **key**. It tells
what the colors mean.

I add my compass rose.
My map is done!

# How to Make a Country Map

1. Ask an adult to print a blank map of your country.
2. Research where places are located in your country.
3. Write in the labels for important locations in your country.
4. Color the locations you have visited in one color. Color the locations you want to visit in a different color.
5. Make a key to explain the colors.
6. Add a compass rose.

# Fun Facts

- The United States started with 13 states. The country now has 50.

- Alaska has more land than any other state.

- Rhode Island has less land than any other state.

- More people live in Rhode Island than in Alaska!

- Washington, D.C., is a small area on the East Coast. It is not a state. It is our country's **capital**.

# Glossary

**blank** – not filled in with details

**capital** – a place where the government is based

**compass rose** – a drawing showing the directions on a map

**key** – the part of a map that explains the meaning of certain colors or symbols on the map

**location** – where something is

# Index